MW01075843

Holy Week

Holy Week

The Week That Changed the World

R.C. SPROUL

 LIGONIER MINISTRIES

Holy Week: The Week That Changed the World
© 2025 by the R.C. Sproul Trust

Published by Ligonier Ministries
421 Ligonier Court, Sanford, FL 32771
Ligonier.org

Printed in China
Amity Printing Company
0000225

978-1-64289-664-0 (Hardcover)
978-1-64289-665-7 (ePub)

Cover design: Faceout Studio
Interior design and typeset: Ligonier Editorial

Ligonier Ministries edited and adapted Dr. R.C. Sproul's original material to create this volume. We are thankful to Mrs. Vesta Sproul for her invaluable help on this project.

Unless otherwise noted, Scripture quotations are from the ESV® Bible (The Holy Bible, English Standard Version®), copyright © 2001 by Crossway, a publishing ministry of Good News Publishers. Used by permission. All rights reserved.

Library of Congress Control Number: 2024936526

Contents

Maundy Thursday

I.   The Last Supper 3

II. The Betrayal 11

III. The Midnight Trial 17

Good Friday

IV. The Curse of the Cross 29

V. The Seven Last Words of Christ 39

Saturday

VI. What Happened on Saturday? 51

Resurrection Sunday

VII. The Mysterious Gardener 63

After the Resurrection

VIII.   The Emmaus Road...................... 75

IX.   The Doubting Disciple.................. 85

About the Author............................. 95

———

Maundy Thursday

Chapter 1

The Last Supper

Some of the most important struggles recorded in the Old Testament were the events leading up to and surrounding the exodus of the Hebrew slaves out of Egypt. We read that God heard the cries of His people and that He summoned Moses and commanded him to go to Pharaoh with this message: "Let my people go, that they may serve me" (Ex. 8:1).

We know how that struggle played out. From a human standpoint, it appeared to be an ongoing conflict between Pharaoh, who was the most powerful ruler in the world, and Moses, who was a lonely prophet from the Midianite wilderness. But the Scriptures make clear that this struggle was not ultimately between Moses and Pharaoh. Rather, it was between Pharaoh and the Lord God Omnipotent. And because of that, there was no doubt as to how these things would turn out in the end: with God as the Victor.

Because Pharaoh resisted and refused to allow the Jewish slaves to leave Egypt, God visited Pharaoh and the Egyptians with one plague after another. As soon as Pharaoh experienced the dire consequences of one plague, he agreed to let the Jews go. But then Pharaoh's heart was hardened so that he would rescind his permission and force the Jewish slaves to remain in Egypt.

God did this so that every Israelite rescued in the exodus would know that his freedom had been accomplished through His power. One by one, the plagues came, and with each plague, Pharaoh refused to relent. This continued until the final plague, in which God announced that He would send His avenging angel, the destroyer, to pour out His wrath on the Egyptians and on the house of Pharaoh by cursing them in an unprecedented manner: He would kill the firstborn of every Egyptian family, including their servants and their livestock.

By contrast, God told the Jews that the angel of death would not enter their homes if they took a lamb without blemish, killed it, dipped a rod of hyssop into the lamb's blood, and put that blood on the doorposts of their homes. Then when the angel of death came and saw the mark of blood on their doorposts, he would pass over them and their children would not be harmed.

This was one of the most poignant moment in Israel's history, as the people looked forward to the final redemption that would come by the Messiah. But on that evening, when the Jewish people marked their doorposts with blood, they also lost something. They had to sacrifice something of value to them. The lambs were important to their own familial economy, but God commanded them to kill those lambs, take their blood, and put it on the doorposts.

God then instituted a feast called the Passover, in which He instructed the people to roast the lamb in fire and divide it among everyone in the household, along with bitter herbs and unleavened bread. On the evening of the Passover, they were to dress with a belt tied around their waist, a staff in their hand, and sandals on their feet, ready to move in an instant when God came to set them free.

God commanded the Israelites to remember this event annually. Every year, in the first month of the year, they were to celebrate the Passover feast. When their children asked why they were celebrating, the parents were to tell them what the Lord God had done for them that night when He spared their firstborn sons from the angel of death.

So every year, for hundreds and hundreds of years, Jewish families gathered together and celebrated the Passover meal. And from the time that our Lord Jesus was a little child, He celebrated the Passover every year with His family.

As the last hours of His earthly life approached, Jesus said to His disciples, "I have earnestly desired to eat this Passover with you before I suffer" (Luke 22:15). Preparations were made, and a room to accommodate them was secured. Jesus sat down with His disciples for His Last Supper, His last Passover before His death.

In the middle of the celebration, Jesus startled all the disciples by announcing that one of them was going to betray Him. But something else took them by surprise as well: He changed the liturgy of the Passover. The Passover had been followed according to God's instructions for hundreds of years, and no Jewish leader would have dared to change the litany of that meal.

But Jesus took the unleavened bread and said, "Take, eat; this is my body" (Matt. 26:26). And when He took the cup, He said, in effect: "This is now My blood. Not the blood of a lamb that your forefathers sacrificed to escape the angel of death, but My blood, which is poured out for you for the remission of your sins." Then He said something even more startling: "This is my blood of the covenant" (v. 28).

That night, just outside Jerusalem in the upper room, the Old Testament came to an end. That night, the old covenant ended and the new covenant was established. Jesus instituted this new covenant not at His birth or at the beginning of His earthly ministry, but there in the upper room, and He ratified that covenant in blood the next day.

Jesus was saying simply this: "I am the Passover. These hundreds of years of memories and repeated rituals have been leading up to Me and to My death. My death will be like the death of the lambs of our forefathers, sacrificed so that the lambs' blood could mark the spot where God would not judge His people. Those things were all pointing to Me. I am the Lamb."

This is what the Apostle Paul celebrates when he writes: "For Christ, our Passover lamb, has been sacrificed. Let us therefore celebrate the festival" (1 Cor. 5:7–8). In the upper room, Jesus was saying, in effect, that the following day, His death would be the ultimate sacrifice, the sacrifice that would perfectly satisfy the justice of God and turn aside His wrath from all who put their trust in Him.

When He spoke of the Lord's Supper, Jesus also instructed His followers, "Do this in remembrance of me" (Luke 22:19), and Paul writes, "For as often as you eat this bread and drink the cup, you proclaim the Lord's death until he comes" (1 Cor. 11:26).

Every time we celebrate the Lord's Supper, we lift up the blood of our Savior, who is our Passover. And we remember that He is the One who has made the supreme sacrifice to satisfy the demands of God's holy justice.

Chapter 2

The Betrayal

In 1857, Charles Haddon Spurgeon preached a sermon on Proverbs 18:24, which says, "There is a friend who sticks closer than a brother." Spurgeon began with a quote from Cicero, who observed, "Friendship is the only thing in the world concerning the usefulness of which all mankind is agreed." Commenting on that quote, Spurgeon noted, "He who would be happy here in this world must have friends." He then added: "Friendship, though very pleasing and exceedingly blessed, has also been the cause of the greatest misery to men when it has been unworthy and unfaithful. For just in proportion, as a good friend is sweet, a false friend is full of bitterness. A faithless friend is sharper than an adder's tooth, for fidelity, loyalty is an absolute necessity in a true friend."

Most of us, at some point in our lives, have had friends who gave sacrificially of themselves to help us through difficulties. Yet at the same time, most of us have also experienced the anguish inflicted on our souls by unfaithful friends—friends who, for one reason or another, chose at an opportune time to betray us.

The Bible gives us a record of repeated offenses by friends, spouses, and relatives, ranging from the betrayal of Joseph's brothers to the Apostle Paul's last words to Timothy: "Do your best to come to me soon. For Demas, in love with this present world, has deserted me. . . . Luke alone is with me" (2 Tim. 4:9–11). But in the history of the world, no more pernicious betrayal ever took place than the one on the night that our Savior was betrayed.

Think for a moment about the context of that betrayal. Jesus had just announced to His disciples, "I have earnestly desired to eat this Passover with you before I suffer" (Luke 22:15). Jesus knew that His hour had come. The Passover celebration had taken place every year for more than a thousand years since the night that the angel of death passed over the children of Israel but brought judgment on the Egyptians at the moment of the exodus.

This was a sacred time, and Jesus had His disciples go out of their way to make the full preparation for that celebration. While they were gathered to celebrate the Passover, He interrupted the occasion to make a prediction of doom—one so grim that it shook His disciples to the core of their being. He warned them, "Truly, I say to you, one of you will betray me" (Matt. 26:21).

Use your imagination for a moment to consider the effect of His words on the disciples. What was happening in John's mind, in Andrew's mind, or in Peter's mind? John looked at Jesus and asked, "Is it I, Lord?" (v. 22). The others might have asked as well. Yet Judas knew the traitor's identity. He had already negotiated the price of the betrayal and told the leaders how they could identify Jesus in the darkness of the night: "The one I will kiss is the man" (v. 48).

Later that night, Judas led the soldiers to the garden, approached Jesus, and gave Him the kiss of death. "Is it I, Rabbi?" Judas had asked. And Jesus had confirmed it: "You have said so" (v. 25). "What you are going to do, do quickly" (John 13:27). Jesus knew what Judas was going to do. It had been ordained from the beginning of time. Judas was carrying out his own will and, at the same time, the sovereign will of the Father. Yet Jesus said of Judas, "It would have been better for that man if he had not been born" (Matt. 26:24). The disciples had trusted Judas. He was the one who carried the purse. But Jesus knew that he was the son of perdition from the beginning.

When the Apostle Paul speaks about the Lord's Supper, he doesn't say, "On the night when Jesus prayed in Gethsemane." He doesn't say, "On the night when Jesus was arrested by the authorities." Instead, when he identifies that moment in history, Paul says, "On the night when he was betrayed" (1 Cor. 11:23).

It's one thing to take the hostility of this world. The wounds that we suffer for our faith are much easier to bear because they are wounds to the chest. It is the wounds inflicted on the back from fellow believers that are so painful.

But we have One who is our friend and whose loyalty can be depended on absolutely. The one thing we know for sure is that the One who was betrayed that night has never betrayed, and will never betray, His own. He assured His disciples, "I have called you friends" (John 15:15).

It is this loyal One who sets His table before us so that we can commune with Him. We come to Him anew, confess the ways in which we have betrayed Him, and find a fresh experience of His grace, mercy, and forgiveness. Though we have betrayed Him so many times, He still encourages us, "Come to My table, and I will feed you."

Chapter 3

The Midnight Trial

I n John's gospel, we read these familiar words: "For God so loved the world, that he gave his only Son, that whoever believes in him should not perish but have eternal life. For God did not send his Son into the world to condemn the world, but in order that the world might be saved through him" (John 3:16–17). These two verses are filled with optimism and encouragement. But John goes on to record Jesus' next words:

> "Whoever believes in him is not condemned, but whoever does not believe is condemned already,

because he has not believed in the name of the only Son of God. And this is the judgment: the light has come into the world, and people loved the darkness rather than the light because their works were evil. For everyone who does wicked things hates the light and does not come to the light, lest his works should be exposed. But whoever does what is true comes to the light, so that it may be clearly seen that his works have been carried out in God." (vv. 18–21)

Churches around the world observe Maundy Thursday each year. Many also conduct what is called a Tenebrae service, a service of darkness, because of the events that occurred that Thursday evening in Jerusalem. It was a full moon that night before the Passover. And yet that was the darkest night in the history of the world.

As Jesus was meeting in the upper room with His disciples to celebrate the Passover one last time, two of the men at that table would betray Him in the coming hours: one by selling Him to His enemies for thirty pieces of silver (Judas), and the other by blaspheming and denying publicly that he even knew Jesus (Peter).

Many significant events occurred that night. First, Jesus delivered the longest discourse that we find in Scripture regarding the person and work of the Holy Spirit. Second, He instituted foot-washing for His disciples. Third, he announced His last will and testament, saying to them before His departure: "Let not your hearts be troubled. Believe in God; believe also in me. In my Father's house are many rooms. If it were not so, would I have told you that I go to prepare a place for you? And if I go and prepare a place for you, I will come again and will take you to myself, that where I am you may be also" (John 14:1–3). Fourth, he reassured them: "Peace I leave with you; my peace I give to you. Not as the world gives do I give to you. Let not your hearts be troubled, neither let them be afraid" (v. 27). And fifth, Jesus prayed what has been called His High Priestly Prayer, praying that He might enter again into the glory He had with His Father from before the foundation of the world. But principally, He focused the prayer on intercession for His disciples (ch. 17).

When all this was finished, the meeting ended with the singing of a hymn, and they left the upper room to go to the garden of Gethsemane. Keep in mind that all these things started that evening after the sun had set. Twenty-four hours later, Jesus would be dead and buried. In anguish in Gethsemane, He prayed alone to His Father, saying: "Father, if you are willing, remove this cup from me. Nevertheless, not my will, but yours, be done" (Luke 22:42).

The disciples couldn't stay awake with Him for even one hour. They fell asleep while He was wrestling with the Father in prayer. And the Father obviously gave the answer to His Son, saying, in effect: "No, I've set this cup before You. This is Your destiny, and You must drink it to its bitter dregs."

Then there was a sound of a tumult as a huge contingent of armed soldiers arrived, led by Judas. Judas kissed Jesus with the kiss of death, identifying Him for the soldiers, that they might arrest Him. So dark was that night.

The soldiers had a job to do. It was a matter of urgency that they arrest Jesus and bring Him bound to the Sanhedrin so that He might be subjected to trial by the Jewish authorities. Why the hurry? It was inappropriate, improper, and illegal for a capital trial to be carried out at night. It was also illegal to have a capital trial that did not last at least two days, since it was incumbent on the prosecution to interrogate several witnesses.

But this was a kangaroo court. It took place in the dead of night. The Jewish leaders had to get their decision finalized because they could not execute a criminal on the Sabbath, which would begin at dusk the next day. Since the Jews were not permitted under the law of their Roman occupiers to carry out the death penalty, they first had to convict Jesus among the Jewish Sanhedrin and then take Him to Pontius Pilate for the secular judgment. Pilate would hold court only in the mornings, so all their business had to be done that night.

John 3:19 says, "This is the judgment: the light has come into the world, and people loved the darkness rather than the light because their works were evil." One of the things we read in Revelation about the new heaven and new earth is that there will be no night there. There will be no sun, moon, or stars, or any artificial light, because the Lamb's radiance and refulgent glory will supply the light for heaven. There is no darkness in heaven because darkness is the context preferred by the wicked.

Think for a moment how many diabolical acts in the world today take place after sundown and before sunup. We, in our fallen condition, are by nature children of darkness. We prefer the darkness so that we can do those evil deeds that can't stand the scrutiny of daytime. To have a kangaroo court driven by expediency to convict the perfect, sinless Son of God is not something that could possibly have taken place in the light of day.

And so they dragged Jesus first to Annas. Annas had formerly been the high priest, but he had been deposed by Pontius Pilate's predecessor, even though the high priest normally maintained that position for his entire life. But in the minds of the Jews, Annas was still the leading authority, and they went to him first.

Annas interrogated Jesus regarding His claims to be the Messiah.

When Jesus asked Annas for the testimony against Him, He said: "I have spoken openly to the world. I have always taught in synagogues and in the temple, where all Jews come together. I have said nothing in secret. Why do you ask me? Ask those who have heard me what I said to them; they know what I said" (John 18:20–21). In other words, Jesus was saying: "I teach where there are a multitude of witnesses. Where are your witnesses?"

The only "witnesses" they had were false witnesses who had been hired to tell lies about Jesus. The witnesses for the defense were not allowed to speak. When Jesus raised that question, one of the officials slapped Him across the face and snarled, "Is that how you answer the high priest?" (v. 22). Jesus responded, "If what I said is wrong, bear witness about the wrong; but if what I said is right, why do you strike me?" (v. 23).

Annas had had enough. He had heard all that he wanted to hear, so he directed that Jesus be sent to

Caiaphas, who was his son-in-law and the reigning high priest. Jesus then had a second trial that night with the Jewish authorities, who accused Jesus of blasphemy because He claimed to be the Son of God. Yet even that accusation was a violation of Jewish law. Blasphemy required that a person use the name of God in a profane way, and Jesus had never done that.

The Jewish leaders were convinced that Jesus was guilty of a capital offense, but they also knew that Rome would never execute Him for blasphemy because Rome didn't care about that. So they sent Him to Pilate with the charge that Jesus claimed to be king: "We found this man misleading our nation and forbidding us to give tribute to Caesar, and saying that he himself is Christ, a king" (Luke 23:2).

Pilate immediately understood that this was a Jewish problem, so he sent Jesus to Herod Antipas, tetrarch of Galilee. After that encounter, Herod sent Jesus back to Pilate, and during that trial, Pilate proclaimed, "I find no guilt in him" (John 18:38). Nevertheless, to appease the Jews, Pilate delivered Jesus over to be flogged. After the crown of thorns had been placed on Jesus' head, after He been whipped and spit upon, Pilate announced, "Behold the man!" (John 19:5). The night was over, and dawn had broken. And in the light of day, they took Jesus away to be crucified.

———

Good Friday

Chapter 4

The Curse
of the Cross

W hat's so good about Good Friday? In one sense,
it was the darkest Friday that ever marked the
calendar of human events. On that day, the most heinous crime ever committed on this planet was carried
out by sinful people. Yet Christians still call it "good."

We live in a topsy-turvy world, one in which God
turns things upside down. He takes the most diabolical
plans of people and transforms them into the most glorious workings of His sovereign purposes. Whatever
else we know about Good Friday, we know that what
happened that day was not an accident. Rather, it had

been determined in the sovereign plan of God from before the foundation of the world. All the machinations by the Pharisees, scribes, priests, and Roman government would have amounted to nothing were it not for that divine purpose. Jesus Himself proclaimed, "No one takes [My life] from me, but I lay it down of my own accord" (John 10:18).

Cynical and skeptical theologians have called the biblical interpretation of the death of Jesus horrific. They say that the idea that the Father would give up His Son to death is nothing less than cosmic child abuse, and therefore, these theologians argue, it must be rejected. While they are incorrect in their conclusion, they are right at one point: the One who sent Jesus to the cross was God Himself.

As the Scriptures tell us, it pleased the Lord to bruise Him (see Isa. 53:10), not because the Father took some kind of fiendish delight in afflicting His Son but because the Father delighted in the value of what was taking place. On one hand, the perfect justice of God was being upheld because sin received punishment. On the other hand, the most marvelous and glorious expression of grace in the history of the world was put on display. The One who paid the penalty for sin paid it not for Himself but for us. Justice and grace married in an extraordinary ceremony that took place at Golgotha.

When God rescued His people from bondage in Egypt, He made a covenant with them. In that covenant, He set before them dual sanctions: the promise of blessing and the threat of cursing. In Deuteronomy 28, God told the people through Moses that if they kept His law, they would be blessed in the city and blessed in the country. They would be blessed when they lay down and blessed when they rose up.

If they failed to keep His law, however, they would be cursed in the city and cursed in the country. They would be cursed when they lay down and cursed when they stood up. Once that covenant was broken, the only thing that God's people could expect was that curse.

In Numbers, we find the Aaronic benediction: "The LORD bless you and keep you; the LORD make his face to shine upon you and be gracious to you; the LORD lift up his countenance upon you and give you peace" (6:24–26). That great benediction stirred the heart of every pious Jew. What they longed for more than anything else was to experience the beatific vision: to be able to draw so close to God that they could bask in the radiance, effulgence, and glory of His face. But after Adam and Eve's expulsion from the garden of Eden, God had said, in effect: "I will be with you, but My face may not be seen. No one can look upon Me and live" (see Ex. 33:20).

Every Jew yearned for the fulfillment of that benediction: "The LORD bless you and keep you." What blessing meant to the Jew is explained in the rest of the words of the benediction: "The LORD make his face to shine upon you and be gracious to you; the LORD lift up his countenance upon you and give you peace." What could possibly bring greater peace to a believing heart than to behold the face of God? That tells us the meaning of blessedness.

Conversely, the worst thing that could befall a Jew was to hear the malediction of God: "May the Lord curse you and forsake you. May He turn His face away from you, giving you not grace, but wrath.

May the Lord turn off the light of His countenance in your presence, that you may go to the outer darkness, where not a glimpse of the light of His countenance penetrates and where there is only weeping, gnashing of teeth, and no peace whatsoever." That was the price of sin. That's what we have all merited: His curse and nothing else. All our righteousness is but filthy rags, worthy of the curse of God.

The Apostle Paul, reflecting on that covenant sanction, wrote to the Galatians that "all who rely on works of the law are under a curse; for it is written, 'Cursed be everyone who does not abide by all things written in the Book of the Law, and do them.' Now it is evident that no one is justified before God by the law, for 'The righteous shall live by faith'" (3:10–11). This is what's good about Good Friday: "Christ redeemed us from the curse of the law by becoming a curse for us" (v. 13).

In Leviticus, we read this about the Day of Atonement:

"And when he has made an end of atoning for the Holy Place and the tent of meeting and the altar, he shall present the live goat. And Aaron shall lay both his hands on the head of the live goat, and confess over it all the iniquities of the people of Israel, and all their transgressions, all their sins. And he shall put them on the head of the goat and send it away into the wilderness by the hand of a man who is in readiness. The goat shall bear all their iniquities on itself to a remote area, and he shall let the goat go free in the wilderness." (16:20–22)

Two goats were involved in the Day of Atonement: one that was sacrificed by the priests and one that was called the "scapegoat." After the blood offering to satisfy the demand of God's law had been completed, the priest put his hands on the head of the scapegoat. In that act, he symbolically transferred all the sins that the people had committed in the previous twelve months.

With the sins on the back of that goat, the goat was driven outside the camp, outside the land of consecration, and into the wilderness. Jesus is not simply the Lamb; He's also the Goat. The fulfillment of both animals' sacrifice is found in the perfect atonement rendered by our Lord Jesus Christ on the cross. He was the Lamb whose shed blood satisfied the demands of God's justice. He was the Scapegoat who took our sin away.

The author of Hebrews tells us that all the elaborate rituals that took place every year on the Day of Atonement were powerless in themselves to do anything, for "it is impossible for the blood of bulls and goats to take away sins" (Heb. 10:4). Why, then, did God ordain this elaborate ceremony? He did so to foreshadow the final Day of Atonement, when the Lamb without blemish would be slain and His blood would be given as a sacrifice to the Father, as a propitiation.

Propitiation refers to what Christ did to satisfy the demands of God's justice and holiness. It represents the vertical dimension of the atonement. The work of propitiation is that ministry by which Jesus satisfied the justice of God. When Jesus cried out, "My God, my God, why have you forsaken me?" (Matt. 27:46), He was bearing the curse of God for our sin.

If there's one word that we must never surrender in our faith or in our theology, it is *imputation*.

In the sixteenth century, after the great upheaval of the Protestant Reformation that split the church and set people against people, family against family, and nation against nation, there was one last-ditch effort to achieve reconciliation and heal the breach. The great Protestant leaders met with the highest representatives of the Roman Catholic Church to discuss the doctrine of justification and see whether they could come to an agreement that would head off this fracture of Christendom.

They came close. In fact, they thought that they had made peace until one word could not be resolved. The Roman Catholic Church choked on the word *imputation*. They couldn't handle the idea that the only way that we are justified is by the imputation, the transfer, of Jesus' righteousness to us. At the heart of the gospel is the good news that the righteousness that we need, the only righteousness that avails for us, the only righteousness that will ever justify us, is the righteousness of Christ. The only way that we can have the righteousness of Christ is by its being imputed to us.

That's the glory of the grace of God: not only are our sins imputed to Jesus on the cross, but His righteousness is imputed to us. There is a double transfer, without which there can be no salvation before a just and holy God. When Jesus took away our sins into the wilderness and became a curse for us, the great exchange took place. The curse that was on us was given to Him. The blessing that He won by His perfect righteousness was given to us. Because of His death and His life, we can experience God's benediction and escape His malediction.

Because of Good Friday, we can say, "The LORD bless you and keep you; the LORD make his face to shine upon you and be gracious to you; the LORD lift up his countenance upon you and give you peace."

Chapter 5

The Seven Last Words of Christ

When it comes to great figures in history, people always seem interested to know what their last words were. In the case of Jesus, we don't have just one statement—we have seven. In this chapter, we'll briefly look at each of the seven words of Jesus while He was on the cross, compiled from various accounts in the Gospels.

We hear the first statement of Jesus as He observed the people who were surrounding Him and mocking Him—and, ultimately, the people who would kill Him. He cried out to His Father, saying, "Father, forgive them, for they know not what they do" (Luke 23:34). While the religious leaders who had conspired to put Jesus to death were not there to deliver the fatal blows, they knew very well what they were doing.

But Jesus prayed for forgiveness for His executioners, reminding the Father of the existence of mitigating circumstances. There was a profound ignorance on the part of His executioners about what they were doing and to whom they were doing it.

We know from the Scriptures that there are different kinds of ignorance. In the Old Testament, provisions were made for sacrifices for sins committed in ignorance. In moral theology, there is a distinction between *vincible ignorance* and *invincible ignorance*. Invincible ignorance is ignorance that you can't possibly overcome, whereas vincible ignorance is that ignorance that can be and should be conquered by your investigation.

Had the Jewish leaders been godly students of Scripture, had they been open to the truth and loved the truth, they would have known that they were perpetrating the most heinous crime in the history of the world. But Jesus also asked that they be forgiven. If Jesus' prayer was to be answered, the only grounds on which they would be forgiven was the blood that was flowing down the cross from the One who was praying for their forgiveness. Apart from that atoning death, there is no forgiveness from a holy God. In the midst of the atonement, Jesus was praying for the application of its benefit to His murderers.

We also learn from Scripture about the thieves who were crucified with Jesus. Initially, both joined in mocking Him. They said, along with the crowds: "He saved others; he cannot save himself. He is the King of Israel; let him come down now from the cross, and we will believe in him" (Matt. 27:42).

But then suddenly and supernaturally, as the Spirit of God opened his eyes, one of the thieves said to the other, "We are receiving the due reward of our deeds; but this man has done nothing wrong" (Luke 23:41). He turned to Jesus and appealed to Him, "Jesus, remember me when you come into your kingdom" (v. 42).

If ever there was a deathbed conversion, it was that afternoon on the cross next to Jesus. Jesus gave

His personal assurance of salvation to the thief next to Him: "Truly, I say to you, today you will be with me in paradise" (v. 43). This marked the second statement of Christ on the cross.

The third statement is found in John's gospel, where Jesus spoke to His mother, Mary, and to the disciple whom He loved, the Apostle John:

> When Jesus saw his mother and the disciple whom he loved standing nearby, he said to his mother, "Woman, behold, your son!" Then he said to the disciple, "Behold, your mother!" And from that hour the disciple took her to his own home. (19:26–27)

In the very throes of death, Jesus was concerned not for Himself but for those for whom He died. While the disciples hid in the shadows, fearing that they might be associated with Jesus the executed criminal, His mother, His aunt, and Mary Magdalene were front and center, and Jesus' mother watched as her Son was humiliated and crucified.

Perhaps she remembered the words of prophecy spoken on the day that she and Joseph had dedicated the infant Jesus at the temple: "A sword will pierce through your own soul" (Luke 2:35). When the centurion pierced the side of Jesus after He was dead, He didn't feel it. But surely Mary did.

Can you imagine being a mother and watching your son be executed before your very eyes? What mother wouldn't want to step up and take her son's place on that tree? Mary would have done it, and Jesus knew that. But she had also come to develop a deeper understanding of the identity of her Son and of His destiny.

While Jesus was feeling the crushing curse of His heavenly Father on Him in this atoning death, He could see the agony of His own mother. Out of concern for her, Jesus looked down from the cross and said to His mother, "Woman, behold, your son!" (John 19:26). When Jesus told Mary to behold her son, He wasn't talking about Himself. He was saying, "Mother, look at John, for he is now your son." Then He looked at John and said, "Behold, your mother!" (v. 27).

In His final hour, Jesus bequeathed His mother to John and transferred the responsibility of her care to him. We are told that from that day, Mary moved in to the Apostle John's home, and John fulfilled this mandate given to him by his Lord.

The fourth statement of Jesus on the cross was "'Eli, Eli, lema sabachthani?' that is, 'My God, my God, why have you forsaken me?'" (Matt. 27:46). These are the only words of Jesus spoken from the cross that Matthew records. Jesus was at the end of His life. He had almost no breath left in Him. Death was only moments away. We would expect that whatever He might say at this point would be murmured or whispered. Not so. Lest anyone miss His words, our Lord used every ounce of energy in His being and cried with a loud voice, "Eli, Eli, lema sabachthani?," which is a quote of Psalm 22:1 that means "My God, my God, why have you forsaken me?"

In that moment, Jesus was feeling the weight of bearing the curse of God due to us for our sin. The Father was pouring out His wrath on Jesus, who experienced the curse of God. This was necessary so that the price of our sin would be paid.

As His life was slipping away, we hear a fifth statement from our Lord. Fulfilling Old Testament Scriptures, Jesus said, "I thirst" (John 19:28). The agony of crucifixion had caused severe dehydration, and on this occasion, Jesus exclaimed that He was thirsty.

The church has always confessed that in Christ, there is one person with two natures: a divine nature and a human nature. These two natures are perfectly united and can never be separated. There is never a time that Jesus is human and not divine, or that He's divine and not human. Yet we must distinguish those two natures.

Liberal theologians tend to deny the deity of Christ and leave us only with the human Jesus. Evangelical conservatives tend to go the other direction by not taking seriously the limitations of His human nature. I believe that the Council of Chalcedon had it right when it said that the two natures are without mixture, confusion, division, and separation, each nature retaining its own attributes. In the incarnation, the human nature remains human and the divine nature remains divine. Here, we see a glimpse of the human. According to Jesus' human nature, He was thirsty.

Something more was happening here. Notice how John puts it: "After this, Jesus, knowing that all was now finished, said (to fulfill the Scripture), 'I thirst'" (John 19:28; see Pss. 42:2; 63:1). In other words, we have here what's called a purpose clause, which explains why Jesus said, "I thirst." It wasn't simply because He was thirsty, though indeed He had an unquenchable thirst from a human perspective. But He also said it so that the Scripture might be fulfilled.

In every step of His ministry, Jesus was acutely conscious of the Old Testament inspired prophecy of the life and ministry of the Messiah, of what would happen to the Suffering Servant of Israel. He knew that God had appointed these events from before the foundation of the world. And He knew that all things that God had decreed must come to pass.

Then we are told that very shortly after expressing His thirst and being given sour wine, Jesus made a sixth statement, one of His briefest comments from the cross—and arguably the most important one: "It is finished" (John 19:30). The Greek word translated here is *tetelestai*. It is in a form that indicates an action that has been totally completed. It comes from the verb form of the Greek word *telos*, which means "end" or "goal." Jesus is saying that His work was done. He had drunk the cup of God's wrath. The curse had been removed. He had done everything that His Father had asked Him to do and had paid the price of sin for His people.

That's why the New Testament insists that Christ died once for all, never to be repeated. He was the one perfect sacrifice. Nothing could possibly be added to His sacrifice, and nothing could possibly be subtracted from it. It is finished. If you put your faith in Him, if you flee to Him for His forgiving grace, then you know that your salvation is finished. He has done it all.

Having done so, Jesus uttered the seventh statement, His final words, this time to the Father, when He declared, "Father, into your hands I commit my spirit!" (Luke 23:46). No one gospel writer mentions all of Jesus' statements from the cross, but this was presumably the last one. With His last breath, He made a commitment to the Father.

You would suspect that the words Jesus spoke in the last moment of His life would be hardly audible at all, since He was speaking with His last breath. But Jesus cried out with a loud voice, "Father, into your hands I commit my spirit!" Into the hands of the One who had just poured out every drop of wrath on Him. Into the hands of the Father, who had put this curse on Him. In this, Jesus was like Job but infinitely magnified. Job had asserted, "Though he slay me, I will hope in him" (Job 13:15). Jesus exclaimed, "Regardless of the torture, regardless of the wrath, I commit my soul to You."

His last words were a commendation of His life to the Father. Jesus could commend His spirit to the holy, perfect, righteous, eternal Father. And with those words, He breathed His last.

HOLY WEEK

———

Saturday

Chapter 6

What Happened on Saturday?

Jesus was crucified on Good Friday and was buried that same day. He was then raised from the dead on Easter Sunday. That brings up an important question: What happened between Friday and Sunday?

After Jesus was crucified, His friends asked for His body so that they could give Him a proper Jewish burial. Pontius Pilate granted that request and turned the body of Jesus over to Joseph of Arimathea and Nicodemus. Joseph of Arimathea gave his tomb to provide a suitable grave for our Lord.

This fulfilled the Scriptures that the Messiah would make His grave with the rich because there was no deceit on His lips or any violence in His life (see Isa. 53:9). It also fulfilled the Old Testament prophecy that not a single bone of His body would be broken, so that when He died, care was taken in the disposal of His body (see Ex. 12:46; Num. 9:12; Ps. 34:20).

Jesus' body was carefully laid in this grave after being wrapped in strips of linen and anointed with a hundred pounds of spices. When He was laid to rest in the tomb, Mary Magdalene and her friends stood vigil outside the tomb. They wanted to make sure that they knew where He was laid so that they could visit the tomb after the Jewish Sabbath and resume the anointing of Jesus' body.

Even though Pilate had allowed the body to be given a suitable burial, he nevertheless ordered that the grave be sealed by a gigantic rock. He also posted guards there to make sure that no one disturbed it. Therefore, we know that the guards were there. But who else was there?

I have to engage in a bit of speculation here because I can't be sure of this. But we know that when the women came on Sunday morning, they were shocked to see that the stone had been rolled away. They had been worried about the stone, wondering whom they could find to move it so that they could finish the preparation of Jesus' body. And when they arrived, they saw the stone rolled away and an angel sitting on top of the stone.

Where were the guards? The Bible tells us that before the stone was rolled away, God struck the garden with an earthquake and sent an angel from heaven. The angel moved that stone out of the way, and the guards became as dead men. When the women came to see the body of Jesus, instead they saw the guards looking as though they were dead, and an angel sitting on the stone. When they looked into the tomb, Jesus was gone. But there were angels inside the tomb, one at the head where the body had lain, and the other one at the foot.

What were those angels doing in there on the morning of the resurrection? And when did they arrive?

I think they were there Saturday night. I think they were also there Friday night. Let me explain why I believe this is the case.

Pilate posted his guards on the outside of the tomb, but God posted His guards on the inside of the tomb. The first function of the angels that we see in the Old Testament was instituted after Adam and Eve were expelled from the garden of Eden. God sent angels to stand by the entrance with a flaming sword, posted as sentinels, so that no human being could return to paradise.

Not only that, we see that throughout the whole earthly life of Jesus, He was attended by the presence of angels. When Jesus was born in Bethlehem, the angels came with a heavenly chorus outside the fields of Bethlehem, announcing His birth.

When Jesus was sent into the wilderness to be tempted for forty days by Satan, one of the temptations was as follows: "And he took him to Jerusalem and set him on the pinnacle of the temple and said to him, 'If you are the Son of God, throw yourself down from here, for it is written, "He will command his angels concerning you, to guard you," and "On their hands they will bear you up, lest you strike your foot against a stone.'" And Jesus answered him, 'It is said, "You shall not put the Lord your God to the test"'" (Luke 4:9–12).

Jesus didn't have to jump off the top of the temple to know that the angels were looking after Him. And as soon as Satan left Jesus in the wilderness, the angels appeared and ministered to Him. Did the angels just come into the wilderness when Satan was leaving, or had they been there the whole time? If it's true that the Father had said that He was going to give His angels charge over the Son, I suspect that they had never left Him.

And then, at some point, somebody else was there. The women who came to anoint Jesus arrived at the crack of dawn. Darkness was still hovering near the tomb as they approached it, even though the dawn had just broken.

But by that time, Jesus had already been raised. My surmise is that it was very early Sunday morning while it was still dark that one another visitor came to the tomb. We know that Jesus was raised from the dead by God the Holy Spirit (see Rom. 8:11).

We first encounter the Holy Spirit in the Old Testament in the very opening verses of the Bible. In the incredible act of the creation of the universe, the Spirit of God hovered over the waters, and out of the formlessness came the form of the universe. Out of the darkness, God spoke light. That was the power of God the Holy Spirit.

Fast-forward several millennia, and a young peasant Jewish girl was astonished when she was visited by an angel from heaven. This angel proclaimed what, to her, was a bizarre, unbelievable message:

And he came to her and said, "Greetings, O favored one, the Lord is with you!" But she was greatly troubled at the saying, and tried to discern what sort of greeting this might be. And the angel said to her, "Do not be afraid, Mary, for you have found favor with God. And behold, you will conceive in your womb and bear a son, and you shall call his name Jesus. He will be great and will be called the Son of the

Most High. And the Lord God will give to him the throne of his father David, and he will reign over the house of Jacob forever, and of his kingdom there will be no end."

And Mary said to the angel, "How will this be, since I am a virgin?"

And the angel answered her, "The Holy Spirit will come upon you, and the power of the Most High will overshadow you; therefore the child to be born will be called holy—the Son of God." (Luke 1:28–35)

When Gabriel told Mary that the Spirit of the Lord would come upon her and overshadow her, it was the same language, the same imagery, that the Bible uses to speak of God's work of creation. In other words, if God could create a whole universe out of nothing, don't you think He could create an infant in the womb of this young woman? Gabriel said to Mary, "For nothing will be impossible with God" (Luke 1:37). And the Virgin conceived and brought forth her Son. And the same Spirit who caused her to conceive that Son in her womb visited His grave that night.

The last question to consider is this: Why? Why was He raised? The Old Testament tells us about the Day of Atonement, on which atonement was made for the sins of the people. Animals were slaughtered, and their blood was sprinkled on the mercy seat.

But when those animals were killed, they stayed dead. The scapegoat was sent into the outer darkness, never to be heard from again. Why didn't God just leave it at that? Why didn't God, after He took our sins and transferred them to the back of His Son and sent Him to the cross as the ultimate sacrifice, as the ultimate atonement, just leave Him dead and buried?

There are a couple of reasons that God wasn't interested in leaving Jesus dead and buried. The first one is this: He was sinless, and death had no claim on Him. If He hadn't willingly accepted the imputation of our sins upon Him, He could never have died. But in and of Himself, there was no sin, and it was impossible for death to hold Him. People in the secular world today say about the resurrection: "How can you believe in that? That's impossible." But I say: "How can you not believe it? It's impossible that death could hold Him."

Second, Paul declared to the Greeks at Athens, "The times of ignorance God overlooked, but now he commands all people everywhere to repent, because he has fixed a day on which he will judge the world in righteousness by a man whom he has appointed; and of this he has given assurance to all by raising him from the dead" (Acts 17:30–31).

Muhammad is dead. Buddha is dead. Confucius is dead. Moses is dead. Only One has been raised from the dead, because God has only one Mediator between Himself and human beings. He has one, His only begotten Son, and He has demonstrated to the world the One whom He has appointed to be the Judge of all the earth by raising Him from the dead—something that He didn't do for Muhammad.

But Paul also tells us that Jesus was raised for our justification (Rom. 4:25). In one sense, Jesus was raised for His own justification because by the resurrection, God was declaring to the world, "This is my Son, and all the charges brought against Him for which He was executed are false." He therefore was vindicated by the resurrection. But again, what God was doing was not simply vindicating and justifying Jesus.

He's raised for my justification. He's raised for your justification. Why? How can that be? Because in the resurrection, God not only was declaring that Jesus is the One whom He has appointed to be the Judge but was also saying, "I accept the sacrifice that He has offered." Jesus offered Himself to satisfy the demands of God's justice and righteousness.

Yet God said, "Out of the anguish of his soul he shall see and be satisfied" (Isa. 53:11) because the Father was satisfied. He was pleased with His Son and what He had accomplished. To show His Son and the world that He had accepted His perfect sacrifice given once and for all, He raised Him from the dead and exalted Him to the right hand of the Father as the King of kings and Lord of lords.

The King of kings and Lord of lords is not dead. He's alive. And that's why we can joyfully proclaim, "He is risen."

———

Resurrection Sunday

Chapter 7

The Mysterious Gardener

I n the midst of his sufferings, Job gave voice to one of the oldest questions asked by human beings: "If a man dies, shall he live again?" (Job 14:14). The account of the resurrection in John 20 answers this significant question of the ages both dramatically and definitively.

A record of the resurrection of Jesus appears in all four Gospels. There are no contradictions in these various accounts, but the authors do give different details that provide us with additional information, which is always the case with accounts of historical events. Not everyone remembers or mentions exactly the same things. Therefore, we must understand that no one account is a complete, exhaustive record of what took place that morning. Rather, the Gospels give us a general outline that is enough to raise our souls to perpetual exultation.

All four Gospel accounts agree that it was on the first day of the week that the women came early, at the break of dawn, to the tomb. Mark, Luke, and John do not mention the soldiers when the women arrived. But Luke and John tell us that there were two angels, as bright as lightning, at the tomb. They asked these women: "'Why do you seek the living among the dead? He is not here, but has risen.' . . . And returning from the tomb they told all these things to the eleven and to all the rest" (Luke 24:5–6, 9). When the women went back and told the Apostles what they had experienced, the Apostles didn't believe them. Then Peter and John decided to go to the tomb and see.

They ran as fast as they could. John outran Peter and came to the tomb first, and he stooped down and looked in. Jesus was not there. John saw the grave cloths, and the head covering was folded neatly and placed in a corner.

Let's pause to consider the significance of this detail. Why is it so important that they found the cloths and the neatly folded head covering that had covered the corpse of Jesus? It's interesting to me that when Jesus raised Lazarus from the dead and called him forth from the grave, saying, "Lazarus, come out," Lazarus came out, still clad in the grave cloths in which he had been buried. But not so with Jesus.

When Jesus left the tomb, He left behind the material of death, the cloths that had covered His body and the neatly folded head covering. This point was significant to the early church because the rumor was that these disciples or someone else had come and stolen the body. The robbing of graves was not an unusual crime in those days. In fact, it became so common in antiquity that shortly after this, a Roman emperor made grave robbing a capital offense.

But if a robber was going to steal the body, the last thing he would do would be to leave the linen cloths and the spices behind because both were of great monetary value. If thieves had been at work, they would have taken the linen along with the body.

How did Jesus come back to life? Nobody went into the tomb and gave Him mouth-to-mouth resuscitation or placed electrical paddles on His heart. He was dead, and we know that He was dead from the account of His crucifixion, which tells us that the executioners put a spear into His side to ensure His death. His soul had left His body on the cross. Our Lord had said, "Father, into your hands I commit my spirit!" as He breathed His last (Luke 23:46).

Why did the angels move the stone? Was it to let Jesus out? Or was it to let the disciples in to see what had happened? I think it was the latter. Jesus burst through the grave cloths. He likely could have gone through that stone in His now-glorified, radically altered, newly constituted, divinely changed body.

In the meantime, much activity and commotion was occurring among Jesus' followers. The women had spoken with angels. The women had then run back and told the disciples what had happened. The disciples had come running and found the empty tomb.

For some reason, Mary Magdalene remained behind after the disciples had left. She was there again, perhaps hoping against hope that she would find Jesus, or at least His body. No one else was there. And she saw a man. It wasn't an angel. It wasn't a soldier. She didn't know who He was or what He was doing there, but her assumption was a reasonable one. She assumed that He was the gardener.

She stood outside the tomb, weeping. She saw the angels, and they asked her, "Woman, why are you weeping?" She said, "They have taken away my Lord, and I do not know where they have laid him" (John 20:13). After saying this, she turned around, and she saw Jesus. But John tells us that she didn't know that it was Jesus.

So Jesus asked her the same question: "Woman, why are you weeping? Whom are you seeking?" (v. 15). That's an interesting question, isn't it? Jesus knew very well why she was crying, and He also knew whom she was seeking. He wasn't asking her these questions for His own benefit; rather, He was asking her these questions to hasten her understanding of these things.

Still thinking that He was the gardener, she pleaded with Him, "Sir, if you have carried him away, tell me where you have laid him, and I will take him away" (v. 15). Jesus spoke one word to this woman that would change her life forever. He said to her: "Mary" (v. 16).

When Jesus had spoken of His role as the Good Shepherd, He said: "The sheep hear his voice, and he calls his own sheep by name and leads them out. When he has brought out all his own, he goes before them, and the sheep follow him, for they know his voice" (10:3–4). All that He had to say to identify Himself fully and finally to her was her name: "Mary." As soon as she heard it, she knew who He was. She knew that it wasn't the gardener talking to her.

She turned, presumably to face Him, and said, "Rabboni!" (20:16). Usually in the New Testament we hear the title *rabbi*, not *rabboni*. In some rare instances, the title *rabboni* was used as a title of honor for certain rabbis. But for the most part, it was understood as a title given to a heavenly teacher, to a teacher not of this world, to a rabbi from heaven.

When Mary heard her name pronounced by the resurrected Christ, she looked at Him and exclaimed, "Rabboni!" Jesus responded with something puzzling: "Do not cling to me, for I have not yet ascended to the Father; but go to my brothers and say to them, 'I am ascending to my Father and your Father, to my God and your God'" (v. 17). Mary Magdalene obeyed and told the disciples that she had seen the Lord and that He had spoken these things to her.

Some translations read that Jesus said to Mary on this occasion, "Don't touch me." But another possible translation is "Don't hang on to me tightly." We might guess under the circumstances that when He said her name, she fell on her face and grabbed Him by the ankles, hugging Him tightly by His feet. He would later invite Thomas to touch Him, so there was nothing illegal or ungodly about touching the resurrected Jesus. It wasn't her touching Him that was problematic. It was her not wanting to let Him go.

But He had to go. The story wasn't over yet. Jesus had been crucified and raised, but He had to ascend to His Father's house. He had to be seated at His right hand. He had to go to His coronation, where He would be crowned to the songs of millions of angels, the King of kings and the Lord of lords. So for now, Mary had to let Him go.

We might wonder why Jesus was still in the garden when Mary was there. A person who had been wrongly convicted and executed might have been afraid that someone would come and kill him again and put him back into the tomb. But there was no fear of that for Jesus. We read in Paul's letter to the Corinthians about the nature of this glorified body of Jesus:

> For not all flesh is the same, but there is one kind for humans, another for animals, another for birds, and another for fish. There are heavenly bodies and earthly bodies, but the glory of the heavenly is of one kind, and the glory of the earthly is of another. There is one glory of the sun, and another glory of the moon, and another glory of the stars; for star differs from star in glory.

So is it with the resurrection of the dead. What is sown is perishable; what is raised is imperishable. It is sown in dishonor; it is raised in glory. It is sown in weakness; it is raised in power. It is sown a natural body; it is raised a spiritual body. If there is a natural body, there is also a spiritual body. Thus it is written, "The first man Adam became a living being"; the last Adam became a life-giving spirit. (1 Cor. 15:39–45)

Those of us who are in Christ will be raised incorruptible and will be changed, just as Jesus was changed. This mortal body must put on immortality. This perishable body must put on the imperishable. Jesus came out of that tomb in His new glorified humanity, immortal and imperishable; in power, not in weakness; in glory, not in shame. What could possibly harm Him now? He had nothing of which to be afraid. But I don't know why He lingered in the garden.

Perhaps He did so simply to have this conversation with this dear woman who had come to anoint Him in death so that she might be the first eyewitness of the reality of His resurrection.

HOLY WEEK

———

After the Resurrection

Chapter 8

The Emmaus Road

The account of Jesus' meeting His disciples on the road to Emmaus in Luke 24 is filled with pathos. Virtually every emotion known to man appears in these verses. There is drama, irony, pain, sadness, and glory.

We read that two men who had followed Jesus during His earthly ministry had just left Jerusalem on the day of His resurrection. They were walking a distance of seven miles, which was not uncommon in those days. They obviously weren't rushing, since it was possible for Jesus to catch up and to fall in step with them on their journey. It would have taken them approximately two hours to walk this distance from Jerusalem to Emmaus.

Luke tells us that the two men were deeply engrossed in conversation about the events that had transpired a few days previously in and around Jerusalem. Their conversation included a discussion of the crucifixion and death of Jesus. Perhaps they talked about His trial. Perhaps they had been in the crowd when Pilate came out and declared, "Behold the man!" (John 19:5). Maybe they had heard Pilate pronounce his verdict, "I find no guilt in him" (v. 6). They likely were rehashing and rehearsing everything they had heard and seen.

At that very moment, Jesus Himself drew near and went with them. Luke tells us that Jesus' true identity was hidden from them; it was concealed from their eyes. As far as they could perceive, this was just a stranger on the same road who was perhaps looking for company.

Jesus asked them, "What is this conversation that you are holding with each other as you walk?" (Luke 24:17). The text tells us that the men "stood still, looking sad." Think about that for a second. As this conversation went on, these men relayed to Jesus the events that had taken place in Jerusalem. Included in their narrative was the report that the women had brought back from the tomb and that was confirmed by Peter: the tomb was empty.

You would think that this would have buoyed their spirits—that, having heard of the resurrection, they wouldn't be sad. But the reason that they were returning home in a state of sadness and sorrow was that they didn't believe the account of the empty tomb. This reveals a crucial truth that we must understand: the Christian faith is not based on the deductions or inferences drawn from an empty tomb.

Jesus could have been missing from that tomb for many reasons. His body could have indeed been stolen. But what gave faith to the early Christian community was not a deduction from an empty tomb. It was from the eyewitness appearances of the resurrected Christ.

One of the men, whose name was Cleopas, asked Jesus, "Are you the only visitor to Jerusalem who does not know the things that have happened there in these days?" (Luke 24:18). Jesus responded, "What things?" (v. 19). They replied, "Concerning Jesus of Nazareth, a man who was a prophet mighty in deed and word before God and all the people" (v. 19). They then went on to tell Him how the "chief priests and rulers delivered him up to be condemned to death, and crucified him. But we had hoped that he was the one to redeem Israel" (vv. 20–21).

Now we sense why these men were so sad. They had gone from hopefulness to hopelessness. They had lost their hope. Later, the Apostle Paul would say of people who are without Christ that they have no hope and are without God in the world (Eph. 2:12). That's a tragic assessment of the human condition. If you're without Christ, you're without God. And without God, you're without hope. We may cling to some earthly hope. We may hope in our job, in our achievements, in our friends, in our spouse, and in our children. We may place our hope in all the things that we value the most in this world. But from the perspective of God, we are in a state of hopelessness.

If we are without Christ, then we are without hope. And that's a reason to be as sad and sorrowful as these men were while they were walking on the way to Emmaus. Their hearts were crushed inside them. Everything that they had hoped for had failed to come to pass. Are there any among us who at some point in our lives haven't been disillusioned? Are there any among us who haven't put our hope here or invested it there, only to have that hope dashed to smithereens? If you've had that experience, then you can relate to these men who are packing it in and going home: "We had hoped that he was the one to redeem Israel" (Luke 24:21).

Not only that, but it was the third day since these things had happened. And yes, certain women who arrived at the tomb early on Sunday had astonished them. The women reported not only that they hadn't found Jesus' body there, but that they had had a vision of angels, who gave them the news that He was alive. Some of the disciples went to the tomb and found it just as the women had said, but they didn't actually see Jesus.

For these men, the testimony of the women certainly wasn't enough. The proclamation of the angels would not address their hopelessness. The testimony of Peter and the rest was not going to deliver them from their sorrow and sadness. Why? Because they hadn't seen Jesus.

Listen carefully to how Jesus responded to these men. First, let's think about what He didn't say. He didn't urge them to hope against hope or to take an existential leap into the dark. How many times have you heard people tell unbelievers to do that very thing? That's not how Jesus dealt with the hopelessness and the despair of these men.

Instead, He rebuked them: "O foolish ones" (v. 25). I can't help but wonder, since they had been part of the entourage of Jesus, whether they had been present when Jesus preached the Sermon on the Mount, in which He warned people about calling others fools. To call someone foolish in Jewish categories was not to insult his intelligence. It wasn't an intellectual assessment. It was a moral assessment. It was a moral judgment to call someone a fool because as the

Old Testament tells us, "The fool says in his heart, 'There is no God'" (Ps. 14:1).

Imagine being called a fool by the Son of God. It's one thing if I call you a fool. It's another thing if your neighbor calls you a fool. But if the Lord God Omnipotent calls you a fool, then you are a fool.

Jesus said to them, "O foolish ones, and slow of heart to believe all that the prophets have spoken!" (Luke 24:25). Why did He call them foolish? Because they didn't believe the angels? Because they didn't believe the women? Because they didn't believe the Apostolic testimony? He called them fools because they didn't believe the Word of God.

When the Apostle Paul gave his testimony to the resurrection of Christ, he called attention to the fact that five hundred people had seen Jesus at one time, and he talked about the various postresurrection appearances of Jesus. Then he said, "Last of all, as to one untimely born, he appeared also to me" (1 Cor. 15:8). But the main case that the Apostle Paul made is that Jesus rose again according to the Scriptures (v. 4).

So Jesus engaged these men in a comprehensive,

theological, biblical exposition of the Old Testament. He asked, "Was it not necessary that the Christ should suffer these things and enter into his glory?" (Luke 24:26). In other words: "Why are you shocked? Is this not what the Word of God has been telling us for centuries in the Law and in the Prophets?" "And beginning with Moses and all the Prophets, he interpreted to them in all the Scriptures the things concerning himself" (v. 27).

Imagine being in a classroom with Jesus. You and a friend have His undivided attention. He starts in Genesis and goes through Malachi, and He opens to you every insight, every prophecy, everything that the Scriptures taught concerning the Messiah in terms of His suffering and His resurrection.

When Jesus was trying to convince the two disciples of the truth of the resurrection, He didn't say: "Look at My hand. Check out My side. You're asking whether I know anything about what happened in Jerusalem. I have the marks on My body of what happened in Jerusalem. I was the One they put in that tomb. I was the One who rose from the dead."

Instead, He took them to the Scripture. In the upper room, on the night on which He was betrayed, He prayed earnestly for His disciples and for all who would believe in Him through their word. He prayed, "Sanctify them in the truth; your word is truth" (John 17:17). That's an interesting concept in a culture given to relativism. The biblical concept of truth is that which corresponds to reality, that which has no deceitfulness associated with it. So when Jesus communicated to these two men, He communicated God's Word of truth.

When they drew near to the village, Jesus indicated that He was intending to go farther, "but they urged him strongly, saying, 'Stay with us, for it is toward evening and the day is now far spent'" (Luke 24:29). So He agreed to stay with them. As He sat at the table with them, He took bread, blessed it, broke it, and gave it to them. Then their eyes were opened, and they recognized Him. He then vanished from their sight.

They exclaimed to each other, "Did not our hearts burn within us while he talked to us on the road, while he opened to us the Scriptures?" (v. 32). They rose that very hour to go back to Jerusalem, another seven-mile journey. "We have to go back. We can't stay at home. We have to go back and tell the rest of the disciples what we have just experienced, that we have seen the risen Christ. Let's go!"

Cleopas and his friend immediately left for the journey back to Jerusalem. But notice what they said at the table. They didn't say, "Did not our hearts burn within us as He broke bread with us?" They didn't say, "Did not our hearts burn within us when we recognized Him?" Instead, they said, "Did not our hearts burn within us while he talked to us on the road, while he opened to us the Scriptures?" (v. 32).

Under Jesus' tutelage as He taught the Scriptures, these men whose hearts had been crushed were now on fire. Instead of being unbelieving, they were believing. The hardness of their hearts had been changed. The stiffness of their necks had been removed. They had been without faith but now were filled with faith—because "faith comes from hearing, and hearing through the word of Christ" (Rom. 10:17).

Chapter 9

The Doubting Disciple

After Jesus was raised from the dead, He appeared to the women at the tomb, and they sped to tell the other disciples that Jesus was alive. Peter and John raced to the tomb to confirm what the women had said, and when they were certain of its truth, they communicated their findings to the rest of the disciples. When the disciples were gathered in the upper room, Jesus Himself appeared to ten of them. But for some reason, Thomas was not there. He missed out.

When Thomas' friends told him that they had seen Jesus, he didn't believe them. He said that unless he saw the imprint of the nails in His hands and the hole in His side where the soldier had thrust his spear, he would not believe. The Bible doesn't tell us why Thomas was so filled with doubt. He was probably not a skeptic by nature. Yet here we find him expressing skepticism and cynicism.

The cheapest way to be seen as an intellectual is to play the role of the cynic. That way, one can be considered as being above the fray and remain aloof. But cynics are a dime a dozen. Anyone can be a cynic. Cynics never actually contribute anything to the pursuit of truth. The ancient cynics of Greece professed a motto: "All statements are false."

You don't have to be a prodigious scholar like Plato or Socrates to see the folly of such a statement. It doesn't take a rocket scientist to see that if all statements are false, the statement "all statements are false" must also be false. The motto falls under its own weight. But we find that sort of thing with the modern relativists who tell us, "There are no absolutes." What they're trying to say is that there are no absolutes except the absolute that there are absolutely no absolutes. How silly.

Thomas was probably not like that, but it's still puzzling why he was so skeptical. After all, he had sat at the feet of Jesus for three years. He had been a witness to the miracles that Christ had performed. He was well aware that Jesus had raised from the dead the widow of Nain's son and that He had raised from the dead the beloved daughter of Jairus. Certainly, he knew that Jesus had gone to Bethany and called Lazarus out of the tomb after he had been in a state of corruption for four days.

You would think that someone who had seen those remarkable displays of Christ's power over death would be more apt to believe the testimony of the disciples. So why would he doubt? We can only speculate, but perhaps it was for this reason: he had put everything he hoped for in Christ.

Thomas had left everything behind. He had followed Jesus every single day. He had hung on every word that Jesus spoke. He was filled with hope that Jesus was indeed the Messiah. Jesus had come triumphantly into Jerusalem. But then, Thomas watched Him die. With the death of Jesus came the death of every hope and aspiration that had beat in Thomas' breast.

When we have set our hopes on something and have cherished expectations that are not fulfilled, we often become guarded. If someone betrays us, we are wary about trusting that person a second time. We even have a saying: "Fool me once, shame on you. Fool me twice, shame on me."

Thomas had his hopes utterly dashed, and he wasn't going to let that happen again. Therefore, he said that he wanted empirical proof that Jesus was alive before he would believe.

There is something ironic in the text. We might expect the other disciples to have run out of the room, trying to find Jesus, hoping that He would appear to them again. Then they could say to Him: "Jesus, you have to come quickly. We told Thomas, but he doesn't believe. He's paralyzed with doubt. Please come and appear to him so that he can be convinced."

Jesus did end up appearing, but it wasn't, as we might expect, the next day. Rather, the text says, "Eight days later" (John 20:26). Jesus let Thomas wait for eight days. No doubt, Thomas was wondering that whole time whether the Apostles were telling the truth. Their testimony seemed too good to be true—but what if they were right?

After eight days, the disciples were assembled once again in the upper room. But this time, Thomas was in their midst. The door was shut. Suddenly, Jesus came into the room.

Not only did Jesus appear, but He spoke. As soon as He entered the room, He looked at His disciples and said to them, "Peace be with you" (v. 26). It was a general greeting. But then Jesus fixed His gaze on Thomas and told him: "Put your finger here, and see my hands; and put out your hand, and place it in my side. Do not disbelieve, but believe" (v. 27).

The Bible doesn't tell us what Thomas did. We don't know whether he actually reached out and touched Jesus. But it does tell us what Thomas said.

With the risen Christ standing in front of him, showing him His hands and His side, Thomas beheld Jesus. And he declared, "My Lord and my God!" (v. 28).

A few weeks earlier at Caesarea Philippi, Jesus had asked His disciples, "Who do people say that the Son of Man is?" (Matt. 16:13). They replied, "Some say John the Baptist, others say Elijah, and others Jeremiah or one of the prophets" (v. 14). Jesus responded, "But who do you say that I am?" (v. 15).

Peter replied, "You are the Christ, the Son of the living God" (v. 16). Jesus then pronounced a benediction on him: "Blessed are you, Simon Bar-Jonah! For flesh and blood has not revealed this to you, but my Father who is in heaven. And I tell you, you are Peter, and on this rock I will build my church" (vv. 17–18). This statement in which Peter expressed his conviction that Jesus was indeed the Messiah is called the Great Confession.

As far as I'm concerned, that confession is the penultimate confession of the New Testament, not the ultimate one. If you really want to hear the words of the Great Confession, you must look at this passage where

Thomas says, "My Lord and my God!" (John 20:28).

Some people claim that you can have Jesus as Savior but not as Lord. You can go to Jesus and embrace His saving work as a ticket out of hell, but not submit your life to the authority of Jesus. Maybe someday in the future you'll go to the next level of Christian discipleship and embrace Jesus as Lord, but you can be a Christian in the meantime. This is utterly false. You can't have Jesus as your Savior and reject Him as your Lord, nor can you have Him as your Lord and reject Him as your God.

Thomas understood the implications of the resurrection. He understood that God had vindicated the claims of Jesus, that God had raised Him for our justification. And he understood that if Christ was alive in front of him, He had to be Lord; He had to be God incarnate.

John concludes this passage in a remarkable way: "Jesus said to [Thomas], 'Have you believed because you have seen me? Blessed are those who have not seen and yet have believed'" (v. 29). If you're a Christian, you're included in that benediction.

Augustine made an important distinction between faith and credulity. *Credulity* describes the condition of those people who believe anything they read and anything they hear without any sound basis for it. They live a life filled with superstition. Credulity is irrational. Augustine said, in effect: "Faith is not credulity. Faith rests upon the foundation of the testimony of God, the testimony of history, the veracity of His words." There is a solid foundation for putting your trust in God, even if you've never seen Him.

John Calvin made a distinction between proof and persuasion. There are people so biased against truth that no matter how much evidence they get, even if the evidence is compelling and the proof overwhelming, they will resist it. That's why Jesus rebuked people in His day for being stiff-necked and slow of heart to believe. They had a bias whereby they were indisposed to the things of God. They didn't want God in their thinking. That's our natural condition. We are, by nature, a stiff-necked people, slow to believe, resistant to the truth of God. That's why Christ pronounces His benediction on those who believe.

John concludes this account with Thomas with some important words: "Now Jesus did many other signs in the presence of the disciples, which are not written in this book" (v. 30). Notice the word that he uses here: "signs." That is John's favorite word for "miracles."

The first miracle of Christ that John recorded was the miracle at the wedding feast of Cana. There, with His word alone, Jesus changed water into wine. When He healed the paralytic, that was a sign. When He gave sight to the blind, that was a sign. When He gave hearing to the deaf, that was a sign. When He raised people from the dead, those occasions were signs.

They're called signs because they're significant. They are signs that go beyond the immediate experience. Nicodemus understood this. He said to Jesus, "Rabbi, we know that you are a teacher come from God, for no one can do these signs that you do unless God is with him" (John 3:2).

After John tells us that Jesus did many other signs that John did not include in his gospel, he concludes by saying, "But these are written so that you may believe that Jesus is the Christ, the Son of God" (20:31). John tells us his purpose. He shares his agenda. He has written his gospel to persuade people that Jesus is the Messiah and that He is the Son of God.

He continues with another purpose clause: "and that by believing you may have life in his name" (v. 31). John wrote not only that people would believe that Jesus is the Messiah. He wrote these things so that by believing, people might have life in His name. Do you remember when Jesus spoke those words? In John 10:10, Jesus declared, "I came that they may have life and have it abundantly." That might puzzle you. You might think: "Wait a minute. I'm already alive." But while we all have biological life, we don't all have the life that Jesus is talking about here.

People around the world right now don't know Jesus and are still held captive by the fear of death. May we proclaim the truth of the life, death, resurrection, and ascension of Jesus Christ, in accordance with the Scriptures, that they too may become those who believe in Him, the resurrection and the life.

About the Author

Dr. R.C. Sproul was founder of Ligonier Ministries, first minister of preaching and teaching at Saint Andrew's Chapel in Sanford, Fla., first president of Reformation Bible College, executive editor of *Tabletalk* magazine, and general editor of the *Reformation Study Bible*. His radio program, *Renewing Your Mind*, is still broadcast daily on hundreds of radio stations around the world and can also be heard online. He was author of more than one hundred books, including *The Holiness of God*, *Chosen by God*, and *Everyone's a Theologian*. He was recognized throughout the world for his articulate defense of the inerrancy of Scripture and the need for God's people to stand with conviction upon His Word.